SELECTED POEMS OF
JOHN KEATS

SELECTED POEMS OF
JOHN KEATS
1795–1821

METHUEN

This selection first published in Great Britain by Methuen 2005
Copyright © 2005 by Methuen Publishing Ltd

Methuen Publishing Ltd
215 Vauxhall Bridge Road
London SW1V 1EJ
www.methuen.co.uk

Methuen Publishing Limited Reg. No. 3543167

ISBN 0 413 77508 9

1 3 5 7 9 10 8 6 4 2

A CIP catalogue for this title
is available from the British Library.

Printed and bound in Great Britain
by St Edmundsbury Press, Bury St Edmunds, Suffolk

Contents

On First Looking into Chapman's Homer

Much have I travell'd in the realms of gold,
　And many goodly states and kingdoms seen;
　Round many western islands have I been
Which bards in fealty to Apollo hold.
Oft of one wide expanse had I been told
　That deep-brow'd Homer ruled as his
　　demesne;
　Yet did I never breathe its pure serene
Till I heard Chapman speak out loud and bold:
Then I felt I like some watcher of the skies
　When a new planet swims into his ken;
Or like stout Cortez when with eagle eyes
　He star'd at the Pacific – and all his men
Look'd at each other with a wild surmise –
　Silent, upon a peak in Darien.

'When I have fears that I may cease to be'

WHEN I have fears that I may cease to be
  Before my pen has glean'd my teeming brain,
Before high-piled books, in charact'ry,
  Hold like rich garners the full-ripen'd grain;
When I behold, upon the night's starr'd face,
  Huge cloudy symbols of a high romance,
And think that I may never live to trace
  Their shadows, with the magic hand of chance;
And when I feel, fair creature of an hour!
  That I shall never look upon thee more,
Never have relish in the faery power
  Of unreflecting love! – then on the shore
Of the wide world I stand alone, and think,
  Till love and fame to nothingness do sink.

from Endymion

Book I, lines 1–33

A THING of beauty is a joy for ever:
Its loveliness increases; it will never
Pass into nothingness; but still will keep
A bower quiet for us, and a sleep
Full of sweet dreams, and health, and quiet breathing.
Therefore, on every morrow, are we wreathing
A flowery band to bind us to the earth,
Spite of despondence, of the inhuman dearth
Of noble natures, of the gloomy days,
Of all the unhealthy and o'er-darkened ways
Made for our searching: yes, in spite of all,
Some shape of beauty moves away the pall
From our dark spirits. Such the sun, the moon,
Trees old, and young, sprouting a shady boon
For simple sheep; and such are daffodils
With the green world they live in; and clear rills
That for themselves a cooling covert make
'Gainst the hot season; the mid forest brake,
Rich with a sprinkling of fair musk-rose blooms:
And such too is the grandeur of the dooms
We have imagined for the mighty dead;
All lovely tales that we have heard or read –

from Endymion

An endless fountain of immortal drink,
Pouring unto us from the heaven's brink.

    Nor do we merely feel these essences
For one short hour; no, even as the trees
That whisper round a temple become soon
Dear as the temple's self, so does the moon,
The passion poesy, glories infinite,
Haunt us till they become a cheering light
Unto our souls, and bound to us so fast,
That, whether there be shine, or gloom o'ercast,
They always must be with us, or we die.

The Eve of St. Agnes

I

Sᴛ. Agnes' Eve – Ah, bitter chill it was!
The owl, for all his feathers, was a-cold;
The hare limp'd trembling through the frozen grass,
And silent was the flock in woolly fold:
Numb were the Beadsman's fingers, while he told
His rosary, and while his frosted breath,
Like pious incense from a censer old,
Seem'd taking flight for heaven, without a death,
Past the sweet Virgin's picture, while his prayer he
saith.

II

His prayer he saith, this patient, holy man;
Then takes his lamp, and riseth from his knees,
And back returneth, meagre, barefoot, wan,
Along the chapel aisle by slow degrees:
The sculptur'd dead, on each side, seem to freeze,
Emprison'd in black, purgatorial rails:
Knights, ladies, praying in dumb orat'ries,
He passeth by; and his weak spirit fails
To think how they may ache in icy hoods and mails.

III

Northward he turneth through a little door,
And scarce three steps, ere Music's golden tongue
Flatter'd to tears this aged man and poor;
But no – already had his deathbell rung;
The joys of all his life were said and sung:
His was harsh penance on St. Agnes' Eve:
Another way he went, and soon among
Rough ashes sat he for his soul's reprieve,
And all night kept awake, for sinners' sake to grieve.

IV

That ancient Beadsman heard the prelude soft;
And so it chanc'd, for many a door was wide,
From hurry to and fro. Soon, up aloft,
The silver, snarling trumpets 'gan to chide:
The level chambers, ready with their pride,
Were glowing to receive a thousand guests:
The carved angels, ever eager-eyed,
Star'd, where upon their heads the cornice rests,
With hair blown back, and wings put cross-wise on
    their breasts.

V

At length burst in the argent revelry,
With plume, tiara, and all rich array,
Numerous as shadows haunting fairily

The brain, new stuff'd, in youth, with triumphs gay
Of old romance. These let us wish away,
And turn, sole-thoughted, to one Lady there,
Whose heart had brooded, all that wintry day,
On love, and wing'd St. Agnes' saintly care,
As she had heard old dames full many times declare.

VI

They told her how, upon St. Agnes' Eve,
Young virgins might have visions of delight,
And soft adorings from their loves receive
Upon the honey'd middle of the night,
If ceremonies due they did aright;
As, supperless to bed they must retire,
And couch supine their beauties, lily white;
Nor look behind, nor sideways, but require
Of Heaven with upward eyes for all that they desire.

VII

Full of this whim was thoughtful Madeline:
The music, yearning like a God in pain,
She scarcely heard: her maiden eyes divine,
Fix'd on the floor, saw many a sweeping train
Pass by – she heeded not at all: in vain
Came many a tiptoe, amorous cavalier,
And back retir'd; not cool'd by high disdain,
But she saw not: her heart was otherwhere:
She sigh'd for Agnes' dreams, the sweetest of the year.

VIII

She danc'd along with vague, regardless eyes,
    Anxious her lips, her breathing quick and short:
    The hallow'd hour was near at hand: she sighs
    Amid the timbrels, and the throng'd resort
    Of whisperers in anger, or in sport;
    'Mid looks of love, defiance, hate, and scorn,
    Hoodwink'd with faery fancy; all amort,
    Save to St. Agnes and her lambs unshorn,
And all the bliss to be before to-morrow morn.

IX

So, purposing each moment to retire,
    She linger'd still. Meantime, across the moors,
    Had come young Porphyro, with heart on fire
    For Madeline. Beside the portal doors,
    Buttress'd from moonlight, stands he, and implores
    All saints to give him sight of Madeline,
    But for one moment in the tedious hours,
    That he might gaze and worship all unseen;
Perchance speak, kneel, touch, kiss – in sooth such
        things have been.

X

He ventures in: let no buzz'd whisper tell:
    All eyes be muffled, or a hundred swords
    Will storm his heart, Love's fev'rous citadel:

For him, those chambers held barbarian hordes,
Hyena foemen, and hot-blooded lords,
Whose very dogs would execrations howl
Against his lineage: not one breast affords
Him any mercy, in that mansion foul,
Save one old beldame, weak in body and in soul.

XI

Ah, happy chance! the aged creature came,
Shuffling along with ivory-headed wand,
To where he stood, hid from the torch's flame,
Behind a broad hall-pillar, far beyond
The sound of merriment and chorus bland:
He startled her; but soon she knew his face,
And grasp'd his fingers in her palsied hand,
Saying, 'Mercy, Porphyro! hie thee from this place;
'They are all here to-night, the whole blood-thirsty
    race!

XII

'Get hence! get hence! there's dwarfish
    Hildebrand;
'He had a fever late, and in the fit
'He cursed thee and thine, both house and land:
'Then there's that old Lord Maurice, not a whit
'More tame for his gray hairs – Alas me! flit!
'Flit like a ghost away.' – 'Ah, Gossip dear,

'We're safe enough; here in this arm-chair sit,
'And tell me how' – 'Good Saints! not here, not here;
'Follow me, child, or else these stones will be thy bier.'

XIII

He followed through a lowly arched way,
Brushing the cobwebs with his lofty plume,
And as she mutter'd 'Well-a – well-a-day!'
He found him in a little moonlight room,
Pale, lattic'd, chill, and silent as a tomb.
'Now tell me where is Madeline,' said he,
'O tell me, Angela, by the holy loom
'Which none but secret sisterhood may see,
'When they St. Agnes' wool are weaving piously.'

XIV

'St. Agnes! Ah! it is St. Agnes' Eve –
'Yet men will murder upon holy days:
'Thou must hold water in a witch's sieve,
'And be liege-lord of all the Elves and Fays,
'To venture so: it fills me with amaze
'To see thee, Porphyro! – St. Agnes' Eve!
'God's help! my lady fair the conjuror plays
'This very night: good angels her deceive!
'But let me laugh awhile, I've mickle time to
     grieve.'

XV

Feebly she laugheth in the languid moon,
    While Porphyro upon her face doth look,
    Like puzzled urchin on an aged crone
    Who keepeth clos'd a wond'rous riddle-book,
    As spectacled she sits in chimney nook.
    But soon his eyes grew brilliant, when she told
    His lady's purpose; and he scarce could brook
    Tears, at the thought of those enchantments cold,
And Madeline asleep in lap of legends old.

XVI

Sudden a thought came like a full-blown rose,
    Flushing his brow, and in his pained heart
    Made purple riot: then doth he propose
    A stratagem, that makes the beldame start:
    'A cruel man and impious thou art:
    'Sweet lady, let her pray, and sleep, and dream
    'Alone with her good angels, far apart
    'From wicked men like thee. Go, go! – I deem
'Thou canst not surely be the same that thou didst
        seem.'

XVII

'I will not harm her, by all saints I swear,'
    Quoth Porphyro: 'O may I ne'er find grace
    'When my weak voice shall whisper its last prayer,

'If one of her soft ringlets I displace,
'Or look with ruffian passion in her face:
'Good Angela, believe me by these tears;
'Or I will, even in a moment's space,
'Awake, with horrid shout, my foemen's ears,
'And beard them, though they be more fang'd than
      wolves and bears.'

XVIII

'Ah! why wilt thou affright a feeble soul?
'A poor, weak, palsy-stricken, churchyard thing,
'Whose passing-bell may ere the midnight toll;
'Whose prayers for thee, each morn and evening,
'Were never miss'd.' – Thus plaining, doth she bring
A gentler speech from burning Porphyro;
So woful, and of such deep sorrowing,
That Angela gives promise she will do
Whatever he shall wish, betide her weal or woe.

XIX

Which was, to lead him, in close secrecy,
Even to Madeline's chamber, and there hide
Him in a closet, of such privacy
That he might see her beauty unespied,
And win perhaps that night a peerless bride,
While legion'd fairies pac'd the coverlet
And pale enchantment held her sleepy-eyed.

Never on such a night have lovers met,
Since Merlin paid his Demon all the monstrous
    debt.

XX

'It shall be as thou wishest,' said the Dame:
'All cates and dainties shall be stored there
'Quickly on this feast-night: by the tambour frame
'Her own lute thou wilt see: no time to spare,
'For I am slow and feeble, and scarce dare
'On such a catering trust my dizzy head.
'Wait here, my child, with patience; kneel in prayer
'The while: Ah! thou must needs the lady wed,
'Or may I never leave my grave among the dead.'

XXI

So saying, she hobbled off with busy fear.
The lover's endless minutes slowly pass'd;
The dame return'd, and whisper'd in his ear
To follow her; with aged eyes aghast,
From fright of dim espial. Safe at last,
Through many a dusky gallery, they gain
The maiden's chamber, silken, hush'd, and chaste;
Where Porphyro took covert, pleas'd amain.
His poor guide hurried back with agues in her
    brain.

XXII

Her falt'ring hand upon the balustrade,
Old Angela was feeling for the stair,
When Madeline, St. Agnes' charmed maid,
Rose, like a mission'd spirit, unaware:
With silver taper's light, and pious care,
She turn'd, and down the aged gossip led
To a safe level matting. Now prepare,
Young Porphyro, for gazing on that bed;
She comes, she comes again, like ring-dove fray'd
    and fled.

XXIII

Out went the taper as she hurried in;
Its little smoke, in pallid moonshine, died:
She clos'd the door, she panted, all akin
To spirits of the air, and visions wide:
No uttered syllable, or, woe betide!
But to her heart, her heart was voluble,
Paining with eloquence her balmy side;
As though a tongueless nightingale should swell
Her throat in vain, and die, heart-stifled, in her dell.

XXIV

A casement high and triple-arch'd there was,
All garlanded with carven imag'ries

Of fruits, and flowers, and bunches of knot-grass,
And diamonded with panes of quaint device,
Innumerable of stains and splendid dyes,
As are the tiger-moth's deep-damask'd wings;
And in the midst, 'mong thousand heraldries,
And twilight saints, and dim emblazonings,
A shielded scutcheon blush'd with blood of queens
    and kings.

XXV

Full on this casement shone the wintry moon,
And threw warm gules on Madeline's fair breast,
As down she knelt for heaven's grace and boon;
Rose-bloom fell on her hands, together prest,
And on her silver cross soft amethyst,
And on her hair a glory, like a saint:
She seem'd a splendid angel, newly drest,
Save wings, for heaven: – Porphyro grew faint;
She knelt, so pure a thing, so free from mortal taint.

XXVI

Anon his heart revives: her vespers done,
Of all its wreathed pearls her hair she frees;
Unclasps her warmed jewels one by one;
Loosens her fragrant boddice; by degrees
Her rich attire creeps rustling to her knees:
Half-hidden, like a mermaid in sea-weed,

Pensive awhile she dreams awake, and sees,
    In fancy, fair St. Agnes in her bed,
But dares not look behind, or all the charm is fled.

XXVII

Soon, trembling in her soft and chilly nest,
    In sort of wakeful swoon, perplex'd she lay,
Until the poppied warmth of sleep oppress'd
    Her soothed limbs, and soul fatigued away;
Flown, like a thought, until the morrow-day;
    Blissfully haven'd both from joy and pain;
Clasp'd like a missal where swart Paynims pray;
    Blinded alike from sunshine and from rain,
As though a rose should shut, and be a bud again.

XXVIII

Stol'n to this paradise, and so entranced,
    Porphyro gaz'd upon her empty dress,
And listen'd to her breathing, if it chanced
    To wake into a slumberous tenderness;
Which when he heard, that minute did he bless,
    And breath'd himself: then from the closet crept,
Noiseless as fear in a wide wilderness,
    And over the hush'd carpet, silent, stept,
And 'tween the curtains peep'd, where, lo! – how
    fast she slept.

XXIX

Then by the bed-side, where the faded moon
Made a dim, silver twilight, soft he set
A table, and, half anguish'd, threw thereon
A cloth of woven crimson, gold, and jet: –
O for some drowsy Morphean amulet!
The boisterous, midnight, festive clarion,
The kettle-drum, and far-heard clarinet,
Affray his ears, though but in dying tone: –
The hall door shuts again, and all the noise is gone.

XXX

And still she slept an azure-lidded sleep,
In blanched linen, smooth, and lavender'd,
While he from forth the closet brought a heap
Of candied apple, quince, and plum, and gourd
With jellies soother than the creamy curd,
And lucent syrops, tinct with cinnamon;
Manna and dates, in argosy transferr'd
From Fez; and spiced dainties, every one,
From silken Samarcand to cedar'd Lebanon.

XXXI

These delicates he heap'd with glowing hand
On golden dishes and in baskets bright
Of wreathed silver: sumptuous they stand

In the retired quiet of the night,
Filling the chilly room with perfume light. –
'And now, my love, my seraph fair, awake!
'Thou art my heaven, and I thine eremite:
'Open thine eyes, for meek St. Agnes' sake,
'Or I shall drowse beside thee, so my soul doth
     ache.'

XXXII

Thus whispering, his warm, unnerved arm
Sank in her pillow. Shaded was her dream
By the dusk curtains: – 'twas a midnight charm
Impossible to melt as iced stream:
The lustrous salvers in the moonlight gleam;
Broad golden fringe upon the carpet lies:
It seem'd he never, never could redeem
From such a stedfast spell his lady's eyes;
So mus'd awhile, entoil'd in woofed phantasies.

XXXIII

Awakening up, he took her hollow lute, –
Tumultuous, – and, in chords that tenderest be,
He play'd an ancient ditty, long since mute,
In Provence call'd, 'La belle dame sans mercy':
Close to her ear touching the melody; –
Wherewith disturb'd, she utter'd a soft moan:

He ceas'd – she panted quick – and suddenly
  Her blue affrayed eyes wide open shone:
Upon his knees he sank, pale as smooth-sculptured
    stone.

XXXIV

Her eyes were open, but she still beheld,
  Now wide awake, the vision of her sleep:
There was a painful change, that nigh expell'd
  The blisses of her dream so pure and deep
At which fair Madeline began to weep,
  And moan forth witless words with many a sigh;
While still her gaze on Porphyro would keep;
  Who knelt, with joined hands and piteous eye,
Fearing to move or speak, she look'd so dreamingly.

XXXV

'Ah, Porphyro!' said she, 'but even now
  'Thy voice was at sweet tremble in mine ear,
'Made tuneable with every sweetest vow;
  'And those sad eyes were spiritual and clear:
'How chang'd thou art! how pallid, chill, and drear!
  'Give me that voice again, my Porphyro,
'Those looks immortal, those complainings dear!
  'O leave me not in this eternal woe,
'For if thy diest, my Love, I know not where to go.'

XXVI

Beyond a mortal man impassion'd far
At these voluptuous accents, he arose,
Ethereal, flush'd, and like a throbbing star
Seen mid the sapphire heaven's deep repose
Into her dream he melted, as the rose
Blendeth its odour with the violet, –
Solution sweet: meantime the frost-wind blows
Like Love's alarum pattering the sharp sleet
Against the window-panes; St. Agnes' moon hath
    set.

XXXVII

'Tis dark: quick pattereth the flaw-blown sleet:
'This is no dream, my bride, my Madeline!'
'Tis dark: the iced gusts still rave and beat:
'No dream, alas! alas! and woe is mine!
'Porphyro will leave me here to fade and pine.–
'Cruel! what traitor could thee hither bring?
'I curse not, for my heart is lost in thine
'Though thou forsakest a deceived thing; –
'A dove forlorn and lost with sick unpruned wing.'

XXVIII

'My Madeline! sweet dreamer! lovely bride!
'Say, may I be for aye thy vassal blest?
'Thy beauty's shield, heart-shap'd and vermeil dyed?

'Ah, silver shrine, here will I take my rest
'After so many hours of toil and quest,
'A famish'd pilgrim – sav'd by miracle.
'Though I have found, I will not rob thy nest
'Saving of thy sweet self; if thou think'st well
'To trust, fair Madeline, to no rude infidel.'

XXXIX

'Hark! 'tis an elfin-storm from faery land,
'Of haggard seeming, but a boon indeed:
'Arise – arise! the morning is at hand;–
'The bloated wassaillers will never heed: –
'Let us away, my love, with happy speed;
'There are no ears to hear, or eyes to see, –
'Drown'd all in Rhenish and the sleepy mead:
'Awake! arise! my love, and fearless be,
'For o'er the southern moors I have a home for
     thee.'

XL

She hurried at his words, beset with fears,
For there were sleeping dragons all around,
At glaring watch, perhaps, with ready spears –
Down the wide stairs a darkling way they found. –
In all the house was heard no human sound.
A chain-droop'd lamp was flickering by each door;

The arras, rich with horseman, hawk, and hound,
  Flutter'd in the besieging wind's uproar;
And the long carpets rose along the gusty floor.

XLI

They glide, like phantoms, into the wide hall;
Like phantoms, to the iron porch, they glide;
Where lay the Porter, in uneasy sprawl,
With a huge empty flaggon by his side:
The wakeful bloodhound rose, and shook his hide,
But his sagacious eye an inmate owns:
By one, and one, the bolts full easy slide: –
The chains lie silent on the footworn stones; –
The key turns, and the door upon its hinges groans.

XLII

And they are gone: ay, ages long ago
These lovers fled away into the storm.
That night the Baron dreamt of many a woe,
And all his warrior-guests, with shade and form
Of witch, and demon, and large coffin-worm,
Were long be-nightmar'd. Angela the old
Died palsy-twitch'd, with meagre face deform;
The Beadsman, after thousand aves told,
For aye unsought for slept among his ashes cold.

La Belle Dame
sans Merci

I

O what can ail thee, knight-at-arms,
   Alone and palely loitering?
The sedge has wither'd from the lake,
   And no birds sing.

II

O what can ail thee, knight-at-arms,
   So haggard and so woe-begone?
The squirrel's granary is full,
   And the harvest's done.

III

I see a lilly on thy brow,
   With anguish moist and fever dew,
And on thy cheek a fading rose
   Fast withereth too.

IV

I met a lady in the meads,
   Full beautiful – a faery's child,
Her hair was long, her foot was light,
   And her eyes were wild.

V

I made a garland for her head,
    And bracelets too, and fragrant zone;
She look'd at me as she did love,
    And made sweet moan.

VI

I set her on my pacing steed,
    And nothing else saw all day long,
For sideways would she bend, and sing
    A faery's song.

VII

She found me roots of relish sweet,
    And honey wild, and manna dew,
And sure in language strange she said –
    'I love thee true'.

VIII

She took me to her elfin grot,
    And there she wept, and sigh'd full
        sore,
And there I shut her wild wild eyes
    With kisses four.

IX

And there she lulled me asleep,
　　And there I dream'd – Ah! woe betide!
The latest dream I ever dream'd
　　On the cold hill side.

X

I saw pale kings, and princes too,
　　Pale warriors, death-pale were they all;
They cried – 'La Belle Dame sans Merci
　　Hath thee in thrall!'

XI

I saw their starved lips in the gloam,
　　With horrid warning gaped wide,
And I awoke and found me here,
　　On the cold hill's side.

XII

And this is why I sojourn here
　　Alone and palely loitering,
Though the sedge is wither'd from the lake,
　　And no birds sing.

Ode to Psyche

O Goddess! hear these tuneless numbers, wrung
  By sweet enforcement and remembrance dear,
And pardon that thy secrets should be sung
  Even into thine own soft-conched ear:
Surely I dreamt to-day, or did I see
  The winged Psyche with awaken'd eyes?
I wander'd in a forest thoughtlessly,
  And, on the sudden, fainting with surprise,
Saw two fair creatures, couched side by side
  In deepest grass, beneath the whisp'ring roof
  Of leaves and trembled blossoms, where there ran
    A brooklet, scarce espied:
'Mid hush'd, cool-rooted flowers, fragrant-eyed,
  Blue, silver-white, and budded Tyrian,
They lay calm-breathing on the bedded grass;
  Their arms embraced, and their pinions too;
  Their lips touch'd not, but had not bid adieu,
As if disjoined by soft-handed slumber,
And ready still past kisses to outnumber
  At tender eye-dawn of aurorean love:
    The winged boy I knew;
But who wast thou, O happy, happy dove?
    His Psyche true!

O latest-born and loveliest vision far
   Of all Olympus' faded hierarchy!
Fairer than Phoebe's sapphire-region'd star,
   Or Vesper, amorous glow-worm of the sky;
Fairer than these, though temple thou hast none,
      Nor altar heap'd with flowers;
Nor virgin-choir to make delicious moan
      Upon the midnight hours;
No voice, no lute, no pipe, no incense sweet
   From chain-swung censer teeming;
No shrine, no grove, no oracle, no heat
   Of pale-mouth'd prophet dreaming.

O brightest! though too late for antique vows,
   Too, too late for the fond believing lyre,
When holy were the haunted forest boughs,
   Holy the air, the water, and the fire;
Yet even in these days so far retir'd
   From happy pieties, thy lucent fans,
   Fluttering among the faint Olympians,
I see, and sing, by my own eyes inspired.
So let me be thy choir, and make a moan
      Upon the midnight hours;
Thy voice, thy lute, thy pipe, thy incense sweet
   From swinged censer teeming;
Thy shrine, thy grove, thy oracle, thy heat
   Of pale-mouth'd prophet dreaming.

Yes, I will be thy priest, and build a fane
   In some untrodden region of my mind,
Where branched thoughts, new grown with pleasant
     pain,
   Instead of pines shall murmur in the wind:
Far, far around shall those dark-cluster'd trees
   Fledge the wild-ridged mountains steep by steep;
And there by zephyrs, streams, and birds, and bees,
   The moss-lain Dryads shall be lull'd to sleep;
And in the midst of this wide quietness
   A rosy sanctuary will I dress
With the wreath'd trellis of a working brain,
   With buds, and bells, and stars without a name,
With all the gardener Fancy e'er could feign,
   Who, breeding flowers, will never breed the same:
And there shall be for thee all soft delight
   That shadowy thought can win,
A bright torch, and a casement ope at night,
   To let the warm Love in!

Ode to a Nightingale

I

M<small>Y</small> heart aches, and a drowsy numbness pains
   My sense, as though of hemlock I had drunk,
Or emptied some dull opiate to the drains
   One minute past, and Lethe-wards had sunk:
'Tis not through envy of thy happy lot,
   But being too happy in thine happiness, –
      That thou, light-winged Dryad of the trees,
         In some melodious plot
   Of beechen green, and shadows numberless,
      Singest of summer in full-throated ease.

II

O, for a draught of vintage! that hath been
   Cool'd a long age in the deep-delved earth,
Tasting of Flora and the country green,
   Dance, and Provençal song, and sunburnt mirth!
O for a beaker full of the warm South,
   Full of the true, the blushful Hippocrene,
      With beaded bubbles winking at the brim,
         And purple-stained mouth;
   That I might drink, and leave the world unseen,
      And with thee fade away into the forest dim:

III

Fade far away, dissolve, and quite forget
    What thou among the leaves hast never known,
The weariness, the fever, and the fret
    Here, where men sit and hear each other groan;
Where palsy shakes a few, sad, last gray hairs,
    Where youth grows pale, and spectre-thin, and
        dies;
        Where but to think is to be full of sorrow
            And leaden-eyed despairs,
    Where Beauty cannot keep her lustrous eyes,
        Or new Love pine at them beyond to-morrow.

IV

Away! away! for I will fly to thee,
    Not charioted by Bacchus and his pards,
But on the viewless wings of Poesy,
    Though the dull brain perplexes and retards:
Already with thee! tender is the night,
    And haply the Queen-Moon is on her throne,
        Cluster'd around by all her starry Fays;
        But here there is no light,
    Save what from heaven is with the breezes blown
        Through verdurous glooms and windless mossy
        ways.

V

I cannot see what flowers are at my feet,
  Nor what soft incense hangs upon the boughs,
But, in embalmed darkness, guess each sweet
  Wherewith the seasonable month endows
The grass, the thicket, and the fruit-tree wild;
  White hawthorn, and the pastoral eglantine;
    Fast fading violets cover'd up in leaves;
      And mid-May's eldest child,
The coming musk-rose, full of dewy wine,
  The murmurous haunt of flies on summer eves.

VI

Darkling I listen; and for many a time
  I have been half in love with easeful Death,
Call'd him soft names in many a mused rhyme,
  To take into the air my quiet breath;
Now more than ever seems it rich to die,
  To cease upon the midnight with no pain,
    While thou art pouring forth thy soul abroad
      In such an ecstasy!
  Still wouldst thou sing, and I have ears in vain –
    To thy high requiem become a sod.

VII

Thou wast not born for death, immortal Bird!
  No hungry generations tread thee down;
The voice I hear this passing night was heard
  In ancient days by emperor and clown:
Perhaps the self-same song that found a path
  Through the sad heart of Ruth, when, sick for
      home,
      She stood in tears amid the alien corn;
        The same that oft-times hath
  Charm'd magic casements, opening on the foam
  Of perilous seas, in faery lands forlorn.

VIII

Forlorn! the very word is like a bell
  To toll me back from thee to my sole self!
Adieu! the fancy cannot cheat so well
  As she is fam'd to do, deceiving elf.
Adieu! adieu! thy plaintive anthem fades
  Past the near meadows, over the still stream,
    Up the hill-side; and now 'tis buried deep
      In the next valley-glades:
  Was it a vision, or a waking dream?
    Fled is that music: – Do I wake or sleep?

Ode on a Grecian Urn

I

Thou still unravish'd bride of quietness,
  Thou foster-child of silence and slow time,
Sylvan historian, who canst thus express
  A flowery tale more sweetly than our rhyme:
What leaf-fring'd legend haunts about thy shape
  Of deities or mortals, or of both,
    In Tempe or the dales of Arcady?
  What men or gods are these? What maidens loth?
What mad pursuit? What struggle to escape?
    What pipes and timbrels? What wild ecstasy?

II

Heard melodies are sweet, but those unheard
  Are sweeter; therefore, ye soft pipes, play on;
Not to the sensual ear, but, more endear'd,
  Pipe to the spirit ditties of no tone:
Fair youth, beneath the trees, thou canst not leave
  Thy song, nor ever can those trees be bare;
    Bold Lover, never, never canst thou kiss,
Though winning near the goal – yet, do not grieve;
  She cannot fade, though thou hast not thy bliss,
    For ever wilt thou love, and she be fair!

III

Ah, happy, happy boughs! that cannot shed
   Your leaves, nor ever bid the Spring adieu;
And, happy melodist, unwearied,
   For ever piping songs for ever new;
More happy love! more happy, happy love!
   For ever warm and still to be enjoy'd,
     For ever panting, and for ever young;
All breathing human passion far above,
   That leaves a heart high-sorrowful and cloy'd,
     A burning forehead, and a parching tongue.

IV

Who are these coming to the sacrifice?
   To what green altar, O mysterious priest,
Lead'st thou that heifer lowing at the skies,
   And all her silken flanks with garlands drest?
What little town by river or sea shore,
   Or mountain-built with peaceful citadel,
     Is emptied of this folk, this pious morn?
And, little town, thy streets for evermore
   Will silent be; and not a soul to tell
     Why thou art desolate, can e'er return.

V

O Attic shape! Fair attitude! with brede
  Of marble men and maidens overwrought,
With forest branches and the trodden weed;
  Thou, silent form, dost tease us out of thought
As doth eternity: Cold Pastoral!
  When old age shall this generation waste,
    Thou shalt remain, in midst of other woe
Than ours, a friend to man, to whom thou say'st,
  Beauty is truth, truth beauty, – that is all
    Ye know on earth, and all ye need to know.

Ode on Melancholy

I

No, no, go not to Lethe, neither twist
   Wolf's-bane, tight-rooted, for its poisonous wine;
Nor suffer thy pale forehead to be kiss'd
   By nightshade, ruby grape of Proserpine;
Make not your rosary of yew-berries,
    Nor let the beetle, nor the death-moth be
      Your mournful Psyche, nor the downy owl
A partner in your sorrow's mysteries;
    For shade to shade will come too drowsily,
      And drown the wakeful anguish of the soul.

II

But when the melancholy fit shall fall
   Sudden from heaven like a weeping cloud,
That fosters the droop-headed flowers all,
   And hides the green hill in an April shroud;
Then glut thy sorrow on a morning rose,
    Or on the rainbow of the salt sand-wave,
      Or on the wealth of globed peonies;
Or if thy mistress some rich anger shows,
    Emprison her soft hand, and let her rave,
      And feed deep, deep upon her peerless eyes.

III

She dwells with Beauty – Beauty that must die;
  And Joy, whose hand is ever at his lips
Bidding adieu; and aching Pleasure nigh,
  Turning to poison while the bee-mouth sips:
Ay, in the very temple of Delight
  Veil'd Melancholy has her sovran shrine,
    Though seen of none save him whose strenuous
    tongue
Can burst Joy's grape against his palate fine;
  His soul shall taste the sadness of her might,
    And be among her cloudy trophies hung.

To Autumn

I

Season of mists and mellow fruitfulness,
　　Close bosom-friend of the maturing sun;
Conspiring with him how to load and bless
　　With fruit the vines that round the thatch-eves run;
To bend with apples the moss'd cottage-trees,
　　And fill all fruit with ripeness to the core;
　　　　To swell the gourd, and plump the hazel shells
　　With a sweet kernel; to set budding more,
And still more, later flowers for the bees,
Until they think warm days will never cease,
　　For Summer has o'er-brimm'd their clammy cells.

II

Who hath not seen thee oft amid thy store?
　　Sometimes whoever seeks abroad may find
Thee sitting careless on a granary floor,
　　Thy hair soft-lifted by the winnowing wind;
Or on a half-reap'd furrow sound asleep,
　　Drows'd with the fume of poppies, while thy
　　hook
　　　　Spares the next swath and all its twined flowers:
And sometimes like a gleaner thou dost keep

Steady thy laden head across a brook;
Or by a cyder-press, with patient look,
  Thou watchest the last oozings hours by hours.

III

Where are the songs of Spring? Ay, where are they?
  Think not of them, thou hast thy music too, –
While barred clouds bloom the soft-dying day,
  And touch the stubble-plains with rosy hue;
Then in a wailful choir the small gnats mourn
  Among the river sallows, borne aloft
    Or sinking as the light wind lives or dies;
And full-grown lambs loud bleat from hilly bourn;
  Hedge-crickets sing; and now with treble soft
  The red-breast whistles from a garden-croft;
    And gathering swallows twitter in the skies.

'Bright Star'

Bright star! would I were steadfast as thou art –
   Not in lone splendour hung aloft the night
And watching, with eternal lids apart,
   Like nature's patient, sleepless Eremite,
The moving waters at their priestlike task
   Of pure ablution round earth's human shores,
Or gazing on the new soft fallen mask
   Of snow upon the mountains and the moors –
No – yet still stedfast, still unchangeable,
   Pillow'd upon my fair love's ripening breast,
To feel for ever its soft fall and swell,
   Awake for ever in a sweet unrest,
Still, still to hear her tender-taken breath,
And so live ever – or else swoon to death.